IMAGES OF ENGLAND

Around Newton Aycliffe

LORD AND LADY BEVERIDGE. Their biography, by Philip Beveridge Mair, is entitled *Shared Enthusiasm*. William Beveridge, author of *The Beveridge Report* and architect of the Welfare State, was, from 1947 until 1953, the first Chairman of Aycliffe New Town Development Corporation

IMAGES OF ENGLAND

Around Newton Aycliffe

Vera Chapman

NEVILLE PARADE SHOPS AND SHOPPERS. (Beamish Museum)

First published 1995
This new pocket edition 2006
Images unchanged from first edition

Nonsuch Publishing Limited
The Mill, Brimscombe Port,
Stroud, Gloucestershire, GL5 2QG
www.nonsuch-publishing.com

Nonsuch Publishing is an imprint of Tempus Publishing Group

British Library Cataloguing in Publication Data.
A catalogue record for this book is available from the British Library.

ISBN 1-84588-299-7

Typesetting and origination by Nonsuch Publishing Limited
Printed in Great Britain by Oaklands Book Services Limited

Contents

Introduction		7
1.	Before the New Town Came	9
2.	The Royal Ordnance Factory, 1941–1945	21
3.	Early Firms on Aycliffe Trading Estate	33
4.	Early Years of the New Town	49
5.	Events and Special Occasions	65
6.	Churches	79
7.	Schools, Teachers and Pupils	89
8.	Leisure and Pleasure	105
9.	Sport	121
Acknowledgements		128

THE OAK IN BEVERIDGE WAY, A SYMBOL. Aycliffe is named from Anglo-Saxon *ac*, an oak. Ancient oak forests hereabouts had been destroyed by the seventeenth century.

Introduction

Newton Aycliffe was designated in 1947, under the New Towns Act of 1946, but Aycliffe's origins go back to Saxon times, when there was a village, a church, an oak wood and a limestone cliff. It was probably the site of two great synods of Saxon Christians in the eighth century AD.

During the Second World War a Royal Ordnance Factory sprang up near the quiet village around its green. This 'shadow factory', a filling factory for bullets, shells and bombs, employed around 16,000 workers in 1,000 or more buildings spreading over a square mile of marshy land. Fed by trains and buses which ferried workers from a 20-25 mile radius to three-shift, round-the-clock operations, it included specially built stations, sidings, walkways, canteens and a laundry. Tilly buses trundled workers to and from their workshops. Mainly women were employed, referred to by Lord Haw Haw, war-time defector and broadcaster, as Aycliffe's 'little angels'. Begun in 1941, it closed in autumn 1945.

In September 1945 the Board of Trade handed the R.O.F. site to North East Trading Estates Ltd, which had pioneered the hugely successful Team Valley Trading Eastate at Gateshead, near the Tyne, in the 1930s depression. The war-time buildings, brick-built with flat concrete roofs, were converted for industry, and some still survive today. New firms set up, and by 1951 there were seventy firms with 3,000 workers. Some were small-scale enterprises begun by demobilised servicemen with their gratuity money; others were offshoots of national concerns. A lunch club catered for starter staff and their families. In 1973 English Industrial Estates Corporation took over the Estate. By 1980 it employed nearly 11,000.

Newton Aycliffe New Town was founded mainly to house workers on the adjoining Trading Estate, from which it was separated by the Clarence Railway embankment. The Aycliffe Development Corporation (A.D.C.) was constituted on 1 July 1947 and the town officially named in 1948. Some 880 acres bounded by the Great North Road (A1, now A167), the Clarence Railway and the Woodham Burn were acquired for a town of 10,000 people, the smallest of the first batch of post-war New Towns. Most of the land was part of the Eden family's Windlestone Estate, with a strip on the south side once being Lord Eldon's. Both estates had already been sold to tenant farmers. It was an open or greenfield site, farmland without a focal settlement or High Street, so a town centre, shops, churches, schools and social facilities would have to be built. By 1948 the Master Plan had been drawn up by the Grenfell Baines Group.

Building began at the south end with the Clarence Farm scheme. The first sod was cut on 28 June 1948 for forty-one prefabricated bungalows. The first house, 20 Clarence Green, was ceremonially opened on 9 November 1948, when the Bishop of Jarrow dedicated the New Town, pointing out that 'A town is more than bricks and mortar. It is a community of immortal souls.' The first parish church service was held in 1950 in Clarence Farm, and the first neighbourhood shops, opened in 1952 in Neville Parade, replaced temporary ones at the farm. By 1951 there were 341 houses and 600 families. Lord Beveridge, first chairman of the A.D.C., described it as 'a town of toddlers and scooters with very few adolescents. In our 1,000 inhabitants today we have 330 children of school age and below, and only three grandmothers.' Energetic in promoting local amenities, he fretted at the slow funding of social provision.

The early plan was spacious, with housing below ten per acre centred on village greens and based on the neighbourhood principle. Roads were named after famous northerners – bishops, writers, painters and politicians – to give a sense of place and history. Early residents had a high feeling of adventure and friendliness, and were eager to start up leisure activities. Nicknamed 'the Pioneers', they felt part of a great experiment, and endured the seemingly endless building operations with wry humour.

The first town centre shops opened in 1957, and the A.D.C. moved into Churchill House. In 1963 the Hailsham Report argued for increasing the target population to 45,000. In 1966 1,643 acres were added beyond the Woodham Burn, and a new Master Plan followed, with the Burn as a linear park. In the 1970s selling to tenants began and the first private homes were built. The A.D.C. was dissolved and the town transferred to Great Aycliffe Town Council. By 1980 the population had reached 26,000, with nearly 11,000 employed on the industrial estate. In 1981 a more realistic target figure of 32,000 by 1991 was proposed. The population in 1995 is 25,000.

This book of archive photographs captures life around Newton Aycliffe before, during and after the Second World War. It recalls the young town, the pioneers and the dream as we approach Newton Aycliffe's Golden Jubilee.

One

Before the New Town Came

AYCLIFFE HIGH STREET, 1907. This was part of the Great North Road or Post Road. It became in turn an eighteenth-century turnpike, the A1 and then the A167. The distant house was demolished to make a by-pass.

AYCLIFFE VILLAGE GREEN. The National School, right, enlarged in 1835 and 1882, could accommodate 250 children. Both it and the Jubilee School of 1897 have been superseded. The village greens of County Durham were the inspiration behind the initial design of the New Town.

AYCLIFFE VILLAGE AMBULANCE CLASS.

Above: AYCLIFFE VILLAGE WOMEN.

Right: AYCLIFFE VILLAGE POLICEMAN, 1881. Address presented with a Tea Pot and a Purse of Gold to William Norman on leaving Aycliffe. He joined Durham County Constabulary in 1872, and became Sergeant in 1883, dying in service at Leadgate c.1890.

TO MR WILLIAM NORMAN on the occasion of his leaving Aycliffe, April 1881.

Dear Sir,

We the Inhabitants of Aycliffe and Dis[illegible]t desire to express to you on the occasion of our separation the very high eskem in which you are held by us, and our deep sense of the loss we sustain in parting with so kind and so agreeable as well as so valuable and efficient an Officer.

During the whole eight years that you have been resident here you have been a most honourable Member of the Force, and we desire, now you are leaving us to avail ourselves of this opportunity of commending you for your very honourable conduct towards all with whom you have come in contact, and the very creditable manner in which you have always sustained your office; the duties of which you have discharged so efficiently and satisfactorily to all.

We feel it to be a very pleasing duty on this occasion to present you with this Address and the accompanying Tea=Pot and Purse of Gold as a small token of the respect we entertain towards you. We trust that Providence will ever watch over you, and guide protect and prese[illegible] you through a long life of prosperity and happiness; And that Heaven's richest blessings may be vouchsafed to you and your family is the sincere Prayer of your Affectionate Friends,

Signed on Behalf of the Committee

Thomas Garry
Secretary.

Aycliffe May 12th 1881.

AYCLIFFE TURNPIKE TOLL HOUSE, c.1970. The old High Street curved behind the green to resume a northerly direction. It was turnpiked in 1745 as the Boroughbridge to Durham Road. The doorway of the Toll House, now renamed The Gatehouse, formerly faced the road. (John Temple)

THE HAMMER AND PINCERS, c.1900. Thompson Boddy, the then licensee, described himself as a butcher and victualler. This lonely pub along Ricknall Lane was formerly two cottages and a blacksmiths. Councillor Albert Guy, a very early New Town resident, remembers it as one of the few places to go to! A lounge has replaced the left-hand wing, and the whole is now The Blacksmith's Arms country and family pub.

THE GREAT NORTH ROAD, 1930s. The view northward from near the Ricknall Lane turning shows the Gretna Green Wedding Inn on the right. The Travellers' Rest and High Travellers' Rest on the left have both been demolished. Today, the A167 here descends as a dual carriageway after bridging the now defunct Clarence Railway.

THE TRAVELLERS' REST, 1930s. This smallholding with a cowhouse and calfhouse and five acres of land was once The Bay Horse Inn. In the 1930s, its sign, just distinguishable in the photograph, was described as 'a horse carved in relief, with its legs bent in a most peculiar and unaccountable attitude'.

HIGH TRAVELLERS' REST, early 1960s. A terrace of four houses stood at the corner where the old Burn Lane joined the Great North Road. Curiously, three were built of the local cream-coloured dolomite (magnesian limestone), probably from Aycliffe Quarry, but the end one, right, was of sandstone. (Vera Chapman)

THE GRETNA GREEN WEDDING INN, 1957. The name recalls the elopment in 1772 of John Scott, later made 1st Earl of Eldon, with Elizabeth Surtees. His descendants, Earls of Eldon, owned lands on this side of the Great North Road in Preston-le-Skerne township. (Ken Holliday)

Right: A RURAL CORNER, 1975. Kelly and Jacko enjoyed Sun Close, where Central Avenue joins the Great North Road (A167). It is now built over as St Oswald's Court and St Oswald's Walk. (Alex Bell)

Below: WOODHAM FARM, 1930s. The 156-acre farm was bounded by the Great North Road and overlooked the Woodham Burn, seen in the foreground. It had byres for over thirty cows and stables for six horses, but is now an equestrian centre. Ancient Woodham village declined during the later nineteenth century. Across the Burn is Woodham Comprehensive School.

WINDLESTONE HALL, 1905. Built by Sir Robert Johnson Eden in 1834 to the designs of Ignatius Bonomi and lavishly landscaped, the Hall presided over an estate of some 4,000 acres. This was sold in lots in 1936, mainly to tenants. Part of the estate was bought from the new owners for the first phase of the New Town. The sheaves of corn on the Town's Heraldic Shield are taken from the Arms of the Eden family.

BLUE BELLS, 1930s. This 10-acre smallholding at the corner of old Middridge Lane and the newer Greenfield Way has been demolished. It is remembered in nearby road names.

GREENFIELD FARM, c.1915. The Wheldon family farmed 200 acres here from the beginning of this century. There were six sons and five daughters: Zilpah, Elizabeth, Ted, Albert, Will, Robert, Mary, Sydney, Dorothy, David and Gladys. Gladys identifies from left to right: her mother, grandmother, herself (eleven years old), sister and father. Her father bought the first self-binder harvesting machine in the district. Greenfield Comprehensive School is now on the exact site of this 200-year-old farmhouse

GREENFIELD FARM STACKYARD, c.1918. Gladys, on the right, became a teacher and wrote children's books as Gladys O'Connor. Her book A *Far-Off Bell* recalls her childhood life at the farm and at Middridge village school. She remembers elms, oaks and ash, wild roses and honeysuckle and several streams and ponds with frogs and flag (wild iris). Her sister, centre, was a land girl in the First World War. One brother was killed in 1919 when a horse and loaded cart ran away, hit a gatepost and overturned.

LOW MOOR FARM, SIMPASTURE. There was a small hamlet at Simpasture. Low Moor was farmed by Mr and Mrs Matthew Dent. The buildings lingered on opposite The Iron Horse, sited between the row of four new Simpasture Gate shops and the end of Lowery Road. Simpasture Court is now on its site.

FINCHALE FARM, SIMPASTURE. Note the solid plank door and sideways sliding 'Yorkshire' sash windows. Finchale was farmed by Mr and Mrs Joe Nattrass. They moved to Well House Farm near by and left the district on retirement. The site is now The Iron Horse public house. Land was purchased for the New Town by agreement, but farmers were able to continue cultivating until the land was actually needed for building.

CLARENCE COTTAGES, SIMPASTURE. These one-storey cottages were raised to two storeys around 1927-28. On the left lived Mr and Mrs William Lawe, retired farmers, once at Woodham Grange Farm. Their daughter Laura and her husband Moses Stevens lived on the right. Laura Stevens, widowed from 1936, sold cigarettes and tobacco to local farmers, and did dressmaking. She set up the first New Town shop at nearby Clarence Farm (page 56). A block of flats on Dixon Road-Finchale Road corner now occupies the site. The meet is the South Durham Hunt.

WELL HOUSE FARM. This was sited above an old quarry on the south bank of Woodham Burn, just east of Burn Lane, and was farmed by Joe and Laura Nattrass after they had left Finchale Farm.

STONE SLEEPERS. The route of the Stockton and Darlington Railway (1825) skirts the edge of the New Town alongside Greenfield Way. Original stone sleepers still lie *in situ* near Newton Aycliffe station. A stone railway bridge which gave access to Simpasture Farm from Moor Lane is preserved near the Oak Leaf Sports Complex. (Ben Hardaker)

THE CLARENCE RAILWAY OR SIMPASTURE LINE. This branched off the S&DR at Simpasture. In 1915, at the height of the coal trade, the NER electrified the line between Shildon and Newport Sidings in Middlesborough. Huge quantities of coal and coke were carried across this quiet farmland, but traffic did not increase as forecast. Electric traction was abandoned in 1935, the end of a very early electrification. The line closed in 1963, and the Aycliffe section is now a nature trail. Walter Cadd remembers wild strawberries on its embankment behind 20 Clarence Green.

Two

The Royal Ordnance Factory, 1941–1945

Date of Issue 10 OCT 1941

PASS

TO

Danger Area

STAFF

Permit No.

PERMIT OFFICE

Clock No.

R.O.F. PASS (CYRIL N. ROYLE). The Second World War filling factory for bullets, shells and bombs occupied a vast site adjoining the Clarence Railway. Around 16,000, mainly women, were employed in three shifts over 24 hours, ferried in by train and bus over a twenty-mile radius. Around 1,000 flat-topped concrete and brick buildings spread over a square mile, protected by earthen mounds ('bunds') and perhaps by mists from the marshy site! It was never bombed.

Above: KEY WORKERS' HOUSING. Bickford Terrace and Congreave Terrace were built off Heighington Lane, Aycliffe village, when the R.O.F. was developing. Flat-topped like the factory buildings, many have now gained sloping roofs. Police houses, off left, were built after the war, when Durham County Constabulary moved their HQ to former R.O.F. buildings (see page 37).

Left: CONGREAVE TERRACE. Four larger, flat-roofed, four-bedroomed houses with garages and internal air-raid shelters were built for managerial staff. Reginald Ekins, a Lever Bros. chemist in London and Port Sunlight, came as R.O.F. manager to No. 3. Susan Ekins, now Mrs Reed, was born here, and is seen at the gate ready for school. (See pages 36 and 37.)

R.O.F. WORKERS. So secret and dangerous was munitions work that available photographs are of groups taken when the war ended. In October 1945 the factory closed. Women had volunteered or were conscripted when direction of labour was introduced for the young and unattached. For some with long journeys, often in black-out conditions, an eight-hour shift could mean twelve hours away from home.

MORE R.O.F. WORKERS. Overhead heating pipes threaded the site, supplied from a central boiler house (see page 29) .The photograph is taken against a protective mound. Such 'bunds' isolated the workshops from each other for safety. Mrs Margaret Neive, seventh from the right in centre row, remembers eight being killed in an explosion. Some workers had rashes or breathing problems. Hair and skin could be yellow from explosive powders, leading to the nickname 'canaries'. Work was arranged in groups.

GROUP 3. Group 1 dealt with raw powders. Group 3 assembled fuses and filled shells. The notice behind reads: 'Remember. A concealed mistake is a crime. It may cost not only your life but the lives of others.' Front row, seated: -?-, Eva Moss (union rep), Sarah Mason (overlooker), Mr Shackleton (foreman), -?- (welfare officer), -?-, Margaret Walters (Shildon). Standing at ends of front row are, left, Annie Patton, right, Mrs Lester. Third row, centre, the trolley man. Back row, second from left, May Rowell (Coundon). Second row, second from left, Kathleen McGovan. Third row: Gladys Ryder, Billy Ware and May Wilson.

FRIENDS CELEBRATE. They went out for tea at the Odeon cinema in Darlington. In the front row is the trolley man who brought shell cases and filling powders to the conveyor belt production line. Next, to the right, is Sarah Mason (overlooker of all shops), Margot Walters (Shildon) and Edith Bramley (now Mrs Johnson). Also in the picture are Gladys Ryder (Middlesbrough), May Wilson (Middlesbrough) and Ivy Plant (W. Hartlepool).

A TRIP TO SCARBOROUGH. Girls from Group 8, which made large bombs, celebrate the end of the war in August 1945. From the left are Ena Brooksbank, Margaret and Ann Cook (sisters), Mary Mc?, and Vera Campbell. Ann, now Mrs Hutchinson, travelled from Wheatley Hill by bus. She began in 1943 in Group 6, where smoke bombs for ships and tanks were made, and later moved to Group 8. She recalls that eleven were killed in a factory explosion towards the end of the war. Many suffered minor personal accidents.

R.O.F. WOMEN IN MUFTI. Front row, third from left, Mrs B. Little. At work strict safety rules were imposed. At the shifting house, outdoor clothing, shoes, cigarettes, matches and anything metallic had to be left on the 'dirty side'. On the 'clean side', overalls and rubber shoes were donned and cloth triangles tied into turbans with a colour to identify the shift. Working clothes had to be washed at the factory laundry. Everywhere was kept clean. Out of doors, elevated clearways of hard, smooth tar were erected to eliminate friction. (See page 36.)

SERVICE ENGINEERING DEPARTMENT. This was mainly drawing office work. Some factory jobs done originally by hand were later done with machinery. Back row, third from left, Mr H.F. Chippendale.

THE STORES OFFICE. Edna Rees, back row, fourth from right, (now Mrs Chippendale) did paper work at the stores, travelling from Darlington by train to Heighington station where a long platform was built for R.O.F. trains. She enjoyed occasional dances in one of the canteens. Back row, left hand end, Mrs Ann Stewart. Centre row, seventh from left, Ruth Wykes, eleventh Joan Pattinson. Front row, centre, Mr G. Black and Mr F. Jones, third from right hand end, Vera Rickaby, right end, Mr Dennis. Others who signed on the back were D. Wibbs, Edna Hope, G.A. Reed, M. Jackson, ? Davidson, Vera Smith, D. Dowson, M. Snowdon, ? Wood, M. Donald, Irene Gill, D. Duncan, Judy Williams, R. Cottle, D.E. Curry, J. Watson and Joan Potts.

Above: CANTEEN STAFF. Not all are present outside 10G5, the Main Canteen, sited opposite present-day Tallents Engineering works. Here were the kitchens, vegetable preparation and cooking, with an emergency food store beneath. There were 150 canteen staff and 14 satellite canteens. Many staff went to R.O.F. Leeds after Aycliffe closed. Front row, fifth from left, Katherine Murphy, Shildon, manager's secretary; second row, seventh from left, Mr Kell, stores manager and ex-police officer from Nevilles Cross, eleventh Mr Goodall, overall canteen manager, seventeenth Stella Killeen, a 16-year-old (now Mrs Fowler), eighteenth Rose Coxon from Stakeford, Northumberland, lodging at High Travellers' Rest. Second row from back, eighteenth from left, Margaret Hardy, Shildon.

Right: AUXILIARY FIRE SERVICE. Irene Thompson of Shildon, later Mrs Woods, did uniformed service between 1943 and 1945. She also checked R.O.F. stores. 'Examiner of warlike stores' is the description on her discharge certificate from the Armaments Inspection Department, Royal Arsenal, Woolwich, 19 May 1945.

CLEANING STAFF. Cleanliness was an extremely important safety precaution. Front row, left to right: 'Fluff' ? (Hartlepool), Lorreen Foster (now Mrs Chadwick), Ena Knox (Hartlepool) and Peggy ? (Durham). Centre row, seated fourth from left, Mrs Dunn, head of cleaners, fifth Mrs Simpson.

THE CHADWICKS. From the left, Alice Chadwick (R.O.F. Group 3, 'the yellow canaries'), Samuel Chadwick (Coldstream Guards, at Dunkirk, served until 1945), who married, right, Lorreen Foster (R.O.F. cleaning staff).

THE BOILER HOUSE. Power for the factory was generated here. Note the branch railway alongside. Lix and Werner Wolf, starting up a new factory just after the war, lived on site in a long, converted building heated from the central boiler. Heat went off at weekends! She recalls the hissing of overhead pipes, and 'bund' mounds covered with oxlips and ox-eye daisies. Houses for the new firms' families were later built in Carmel Gardens and Thornbury Rise in Darlington.

R.O.F. STATIONS. The old S&DR Heighington station with a special new platform received workers from Darlington. Branch lines from the Clarence Railway served two new stations inside the factory grounds. Simpasture served Bishop Auckland, Crook and Durham workers, and Demon's Bridge beside the A1 served workers from Teesside, Hartlepool and coastal villages. Tilly buses took workers to their respective workshops. Trains arrived and departed at shift-change times. The A1 flyover was built to relieve congestion at the level crossing. Demon's Bridge station site is now Aycliffe Nature Park. (Durham County Council Arts, Libraries and Museums Service)

THE RANGE. Woodham Burn was used as a firing range for testing the factory's ammunitions, which were fired into the hillside. This 1960s picture was taken before houses were built. The hilltop was levelled off for Woodham Burn Infant and Junior Schools. (Kenneth Cook)

ENTERTAINMENTS DEPARTMENT STAFF, 1945. Back row, left to right: Eric Welsh (messenger boy), O. Graham, C. Powney (films), Jennie Conlon (soprano; ENSA and Service Speakers; now Mrs Harrison). Front row, left to right: May Watkins (poster artist), Violet L. Topp (broadcasting), Marion Davidson (manager of Entertainments and of Concert Party), M. Lauder (films), Bert Elliott (pianist).

Bishop Auckland Townswomen's Guild
and Eden Theatre Staff.

A GRAND VARIETY

CONCERT

WILL BE GIVEN BY A

"Works Wonders" Concert Party

In aid of the British Red Cross and St. John Prisoners of War Fund

In the EDEN THEATRE

On Sunday, Nov. 14th

At 3 p.m.

ARTISTES TAKING PART INCLUDE

CHARLES SWEETLAND
EILEEN YOUNG THE DUNNINGS
KENNETH CLARKSON JENNY CONLON
DOT TRATHAM BRENDA
JIMMY ARMSTRONG
MRS. FANTHORPE AND THE GIRLS
WALTER BERN AND BILL HAMMOND
LETTY DAVISON SGT. WYATT
VERENA BURDON AND IRENE WHAINES
DONALD FRASER

Prices of Admission: Dress Circle and Orchestra Stalls 2/6
Circle and Stalls 1/9 Pit Stalls 1/3 Pit and Up. Circle 1
TICKETS OBTAINABLE AT THE EDEN THEATRE

GEO. WOOD & Co. Bishop Auckland

Right: POSTER, 1943. 'Works Wonders' concert parties were R.O.F. workers who, in their spare time, gave concerts in their canteens and also toured the region, keeping up morale in the drab conditions of wartime. Mrs Harrison (soprano Jennie Conlon) remembers boadcasting a solo and duet in a 'Works Wonders' half-hour programme from Aycliffe. 'Workers' Playtime' BBC broadcasts at 12.30 p.m. on weekdays were by professional entertainers.

Below: 'WORKS WONDERS' CONCERT PARTY, JULY 1945. Back row, left to right: Elliott, Brunskill, Topp, Payne, Ellis, Hammond, Fraser, Hewitt. Front row, left to right: Buckman, Jaques, Conlon, Davidson, Fanthorpe, Young, Philips, Gallon, Hodgeson, Wrightson, Roberts.

R.O.F. DRIVERS AND CARS. The Mechanised Transport Corps ferried visiting celebrities and performers, supplies and hospital cases. Visitors included King George VI and Queen Elizabeth (now the 'Queen Mum'), Winston Churchill, Vera Lynn, Gracie Fields, Wilfred Pickles, Dorothy Squires, George Formby, Yehudi Menuhin, Lew Stone and Military Bands.

DRIVERS. Note the ambulances, with bell and spare tyre. (This and the above photograph Durham County Council Arts, Libraries and Museums Service)

Three

Early Firms on Aycliffe Trading Estate

ROYLE TABLE LAMPS. This window display at Binns, Darlington, reflects the old Town Hall and trolley bus or 'trackless tram' wires.

Above: ROYLE TABLE LAMPS STAFF. Cyril N. Royle, front, on right, developed plastics, lacquers and paints and began umbrella and lampshade manufacture near Warrington in 1930. A manager and investigator of a machine design section at Aycliffe R.O.F., he set up in 1945-46 on the new Trading Estate. He was also a professional artist and book illustrator. At the rear, centre, ? Barbosa (Polish), second row, right, Kathy Taylor (artist) and Bert Langlands (artist and cartoonist), front row, right, in apron, Tom ? (wood turner). The girls were all artists, the lamps being hand made and the bases of wood.

Left: THISTLE DESIGN. Raised plastic work was a feature, with gold edging. Research produced a plastic which would adhere to parchment and withstand its acids and rough handling (probably unique at the time), and translucent, fadeless colours which would withstand soap and water. A 1952 price list details a range of the acorn design, from a 10 in shade at 17s. with a 40s. base to a standard lamp with a 22 in shade at 60s. with a 170s. stand.

Right: THE PRINCESS ROYLE. Bert Langlands (see page 34) produced a series of lampshade cartoons. This lady is Mrs Dorothy Royle! The two dozen lampshade designs included 'castle', 'galleon', 'carnival', 'Asia', 'scroll', 'acorn', 'cherry', 'wild rose', 'lotus', 'honeysuckle' and 'water lily'.

Below: R.W. TOOTHILL'S FURNITURE. The factory interior in 1949-50 was at a very early stage. Reg Toothill and his associate Rye Hall were wartime flyers. The speciality was quality chairs and three-piece suites based on tubular metal frames, with foam padding and a little wood. Each had a removable cover, a highly successful feature. Seven patents were granted in 1951-54 for the structure of frames and covers. Stacking chairs and school furniture were made later. The firm sold out in 1989.

THE FIRST FIRM ON THE ESTATE. Reginald Percy Ekins, seen here with his wife Persis (Perse), was a chemist at Lever Bros. and came to Aycliffe R.O.F. as managerial staff (see page 22). He then began in the old R.O.F. laundry (page 25), his 'Aycliffe Laundry Ltd – at your service' competing with Lily Laundry and Richmond Laundry for large contract work. When twin-tubs came into homes, he set up Spruce Cleaners. He took over Shearex Plastics Ltd in Burtree Road in 1948. He was thrice chairman of the Aycliffe Club for the directors of early companies and their families, which had a club hut off Heighington Lane.

KETHRO DESIGN. Susan Ekins, designer and owner, keeps a check in 1969 as Betty Galagher of Shildon loads from an ex-R.O.F. loading bay platform a consignment of children's knock-down furniture for delivery to Macy's store in New York. Susan (see page 22), now Mrs Reed, set up at the rear of her father's Shearex Plastics factory in Burtree Road, and was in business there from the 1960s until 1971.

CHILDREN'S FURNITURE. The desk-chair and nesting stools are an example of Susan Ekins' ingenious Kethro Designs for versatile, easy assembly and dismantling furniture. The range sported bright polyurethane lacquer in red, blue and yellow in varying combinations, and polyether foam cushions with detachable, washable covers.

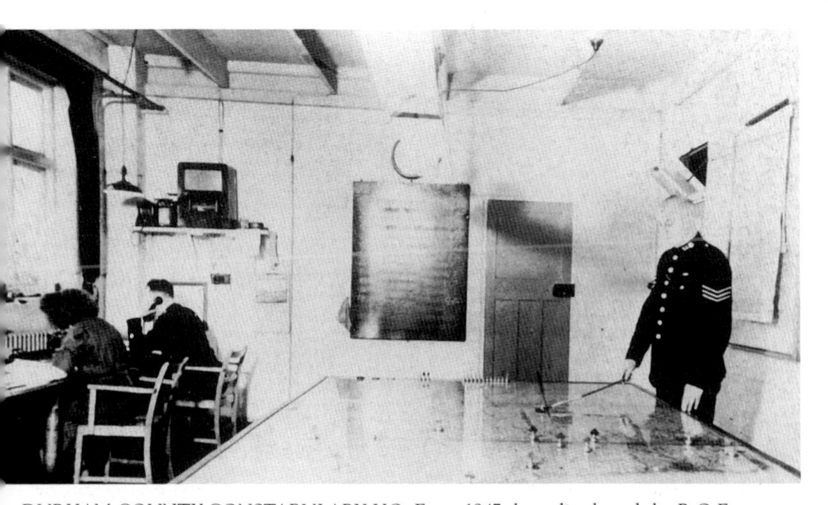

DURHAM COUNTY CONSTABULARY HQ. From 1947 the police leased the R.O.F. administrative buildings at Aycliffe until their century-old County HQ in Durham could be replaced. They remained until 1968. This is the Communications Room for the Traffic and Motor Patrol Officers' section, c.1960.

Left: EAST ANGLIA PLASTICS. Workers in around 1954 included Jack Hawkes, second from the left. Many small firms on the estate were begun by men who invested their demobilisation money to get going. North East Trading Estates Ltd began in September 1945. By 1951 there were 70 firms and 3,000 workers. Early firms included Tallent Engineering, Flymo, U.M.M., Thristlington Engineering, G.E.C., Great Lakes Chemicals, Chemical Compounds, E.M.V. Engineering, Holliday's Garage, Permoid, Pax Paints, G. and M. Kleeman, the Estate P.O. (Mrs Gibson), Swales Foundry, and firms making nappies and artificial pearls.

Below: KLING LACQUERS. The drums are labelled 'East Anglia Lacquer Co. Ltd, Street One, Aycliffe'. The early estate roads went by numbers. This was in Burtree Road, near Royle's lampshade factory.

Above: COMBINED PLASTICS. This is a probable identification. The firm made buttons, dolls' eyes and combs. James Dixon, Mrs Elsie Dixon's father-in-law is in the centre row, third from the left.

Right: LEHMANN, ARCHER AND LANE. A workers group taken in 1954-55 includes Albert Stephenson on the right hand side. (See page 53.)

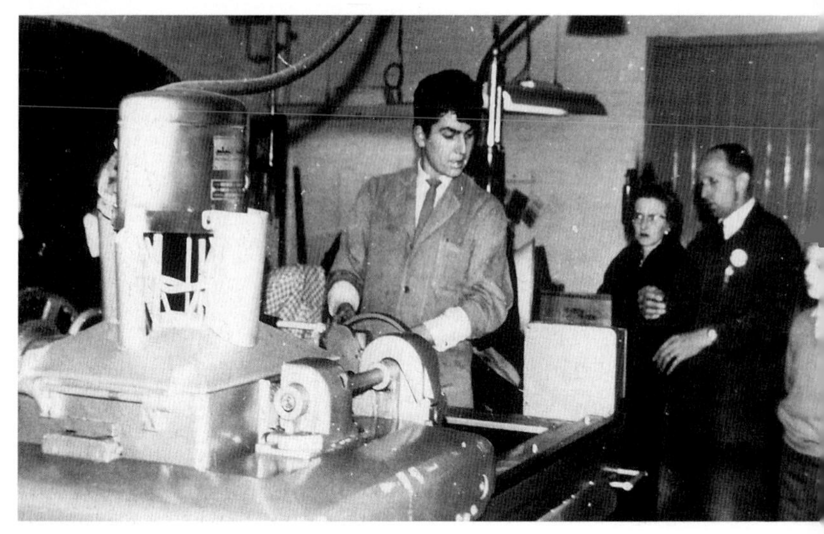

REED CARTONS, 1956-57. Jack Hawkes, on the right, assists on a factory tour. They made packaging for well known goods.

SHRAGER BROS. LTD (FURNITURE). A workers group. Frank Dixon, on the right, came to Newton Aycliffe in 1948 and lived in a pre-fab, No.18 Clarence Green, for twelve years before moving to 11 Gilpin Road. He died in 1984.

S.W. DURHAM TRAINING LTD. The centre for apprentice training was opened in 1967 by war-time fighter pilot Group Captain Douglas R.S. Bader CBE, DS, DFC. Left to right: Douglas Bader, Mr Callaby, George Hurry and Heinz Asbeck. (See pages 50 and 80.)

APPRENTICE AWARDS, 1978/79. Left to right: Trevor Mann, Fred Smith of Shildon (Training Officer for apprentices since 1964), and Tony Atkinson, S.W. Durham Training award winners from Eaton Axles Ltd. Trevor was runner-up for the Log Book award out of 220 first-year apprentices, and Tony won the Charity Shield for the most accurate eight-hour phase test. The plaque behind records that Bader opened the Eaton Axles Ltd Sports Ground where the ceremony took place.

UNDERGROUND MINING MACHINERY (U.M.M.) SETTING UP, 1953. This firm from Germany moved into the former R.O.F. boiler house, left (see page 29), on St Cuthbert's Way-Horndale Avenue corner. They came to manufacture modern machinery for the pits. There were then 108 coal mines working in the region, but from around 1968 mining declined. U.M.M. intended to employ 1,000, and the premises were greatly expanded, but the maximum reached was 625. Like the pits, it has now closed.

SHUNTING AT U.M.M. IN THE FIRST MONTHS.

INTERIOR OF THE OLD R.O.F. BOILER HOUSE. The first welding assembly line is in place.

THE ORIGINAL U.M.M. EMPLOYEES AFTER ONE YEAR. Left to right: Hatfield, Webstell, Alderson, Eaglen, Porter, Langholm, Birtle, Gray, Linton, Rawe, Green, Calvert, Schaw, Innerd, James, Dunlevy, Mears, Whitfield, Dobson, Kay, Sherlock, Richardson and Harrison.

BAKELITE FIRE FIGHTING TEAM. Left to right: Bill Jackson (full time fire officer), Lenny Ebden, Eddie Kell, Humphrey Dodd and Jack Taylor. In training they competed to be the fastest to roll out a hose and get the water running. Bakelite Wareite were into plastic surfaces.

BAKELITE-HYDRO POLYMERS. The Dr Parker Trophy was competed for on a first aid open day. The four-man team, St John Ambulance Works Brigade, is shown with a doctor presumably acting as judge. Left to right: Jack Taylor, Bill Chamberlaine, Joe Hewitson (team captain), Dr Parker and Tom Bell.

BAKELITE. A competition outing is assembled outside The Iron Horse, Simpasture. The Iron Horse was the first pub to be built in the infant New Town.

REMPLOY STAFF, 1975. Remploy establishments were set up in 1945 to provide work for disabled people. At Aycliffe, Alex Bell was the foreman. Of the office staff here only two now remain. Left to right: -?-, Dot Forcett, Sue Greenwood, Sarah Jane Bell (accountant), Leslie Brighouse, Betty Smith and Doreen Hanselman.

EATON LTD (AXLE DIVISION). This aerial view includes the old factory (towards the rear with dark roofing) and the new (in the foreground). The parent firm, now Eaton Corporation, set up in Cleveland, Ohio, in 1914. From 1946 it acquired British firms, including E.N.V. Engineering, Aycliffe, in 1962. The white one-storey building to the right of the old factory is one of the former R.O.F. canteens, and the flat concrete-roofed building behind it was an R.O.F. workshop.

EATON LTD, c.1970. At the firm's sports ground, Heighington (now Highcliff Club), the Mayor was presented with a model axle. The group includes, left to right: fourth, David Bates (human resource manager), Derek Waterworth (financial controller), behind the Mayor to the left, Stan Cavell (plant manager). Back row, fourth from right, Sedgefield Public Relations Officer, second from right, Arnold Snaith (works manager), end of front row, Nora Brewster (secretary to the plant manager). Also present are Malcolm McKee (former plant manager), Maureen Inglis (secretary to the managing director) and a group of councillors.

THE FIRST AXLE. We proudly present the first axle produced here, No. 00001, 15 February 1973. Left to right: Alan Coxon (foreman), Ariel Riley (Bishop Auckland manager from Argentina), Dave Newbury, John Moore, Geoff (Curly) Wilson, -?- (ex-miner from Shildon), Stan Cavell and -?-.

MP TAKES AN INTEREST. A fairly recent visit to Eaton Ltd, probably during a Parliamentary summer recess. Left to right: Stan Cavell, Alf Hart and Derek Foster MP.

APPRENTICE OF THE YEAR. Group Captain Douglas Bader CBE, DS, DFC, presents the Award for 1979 to Stephen Bird at Eaton's Sports Centre in April 1980. Stephen also flew to the USA to visit Eaton Corporation's world headquarters and the axle plant at Cleveland, Ohio, and enjoyed a conducted tour of New York. (See pages 43 and 80.)

THE BLUE BRIDGE. The Clarence Railway, built in 1833, became the R.O.F. site boundary and then served to separate the ensuing trading estate from the New Town. When a new road, St Cuthbert's Way, was constructed to lead off the A1 into the estate and the New Town, the railway was still in use. Freight traffic ceased in 1963 and the line closed.

Four

Early Years of the New Town

CUTTING THE FIRST SOD, 28 JUNE 1948. W.N. Davies, deputy chairman of Aycliffe Development Corporation, is watched by members and staff. Second from the right is Frank Hiley and third Harry Bilton.

AYCLIFFE DEVELOPMENT CORPORATION FINANCE DEPARTMENT. Staff were photographed in July 1948 outside their offices. They later moved to Churchill House and the site is now the RAF Association's Club. The Corporation was constituted on 1 July 1947, and assigned 867 acres bounded by the Clarence Railway, the A1 and the Woodham Burn, mainly to house workers on the estate. The target population was 10,000. The Master Plan was drawn up in 1948 by the Grenfell Baines Group.

THE FIRST HOUSING: PRE-FABS. The Clarence Farm Scheme for forty-one prefabricated bungalows in Clarence Green and Travellers Green was for key workers in the Trading Estate and Development Corporation. The Dedication Service for the New Town by the Bishop of Jarrow was held on 9 November 1948. Lord Beveridge handed the key of 20 Clarence Green, the first house to be occupied, to Mr and Mrs D.G. Perry and planted an oak on the Green. The first library was at 9 Clarence Green, served by Durham County Council's mobile library.

Right: HOME SWEET HOME. Elsie Dixon, at the door of 18 Clarence Green with Alan, one of the first two babies born to residents. Alan arrived first, but at her mother's, whereas Carolyn Corner was born in the town. Elsie and her husband Frank came in 1948. She remembers the travelling shops: Graves Cakes, Bradley the butcher, West Cornforth Store, Bishop Auckland Co-op, Meadow Dairy and J.T. Carey's Dairy. After twelve years the Dixons moved to 11 Gilpin Road. Frank died in 1984.

Below: THE OLD CRICKET PAVILION. Enid Marshall, now Mrs Hugill, is with the children of cricketers. The pavilion was off Westmorland Way, by Thurlow Grove and Woodham Burn. The Marshalls were the fifth family to come to the New Town. Early residents were nicknamed The Pioneers. They endured years of dusty, muddy building operations which they wryly recall.

Above: MOVING IN. W.H. Williams brings a bed-settee and furniture from his new 1948 van into the first completed permanent house. The houses opposite were still unfinished. The pre-fabs were intended as a short-term measure, but are still there, encased and modernised. Mr Williams carried products for many firms on the Industrial Estate. His father began the removal and transport business based in Spennymoor in 1919. The photograph appeared in *Picture Post*.

Left: THEIR NEW HOME. Albert and Lucinda Stephenson insert the key of their new home, 11 Gilpin Road, in May 1952. All houses in the early years were for letting, and prospective tenants were vetted by the housing manager, Miss E.M.B. Hamilton (see page 114). In 1972-73 many houses were sold to sitting tenants. The first private housing estate was built in 1973.

Right: A HELPING HAND. Neighbours Lucida Stephenson and Annie Wilson inspect the Christmas cake baked in the larger of their ovens, c. 1956. Co-operation and friendliness characterised the early years 'on the town'.

Below: A LEISURELY CHAT. Lena Hawkes stands at the gate of her mum's house, 11 Gilpin Road, in 1956.

Above: DAUGHTER ALSO HAS A NEW HOME. Jack and Lena Hawkes pose at the door of their new home, 23 Butler Road, in 1953. In the earliest days newcomers were individually welcomed. With the rapid growth Welcome Parties were held instead. The early town layout was spacious, with ten houses per acre centred round village greens.

Left: DOMESTIC SCENE, 1955. Jack and Lena Hawkes and son Athol relax at leisure. Athol is enjoying the *Dandy* comic. Similar comics were *Beano*, *Robin*, *Swift* and *Eagle*. New Town houses were linked to Rediffusion radio, with four stations, A the Light Programme, B Home Service, C Radio Luxembourg and D the Third Programme. E and F were not then in use.

Above: NEVILLE PARADE, 1952-53. Lucida Stephenson and her brother Jim Wilson stand by the empty site of the Methodist church to be.

Left: THE THIRD GENERATION. Athol Hawkes and Joanna Huddleston marry at Neville Parade Methodist church, 5 March 1968.

THE TOWN'S FIRST SHOP AND PO. Laura Stevens (page 87), here with her daughter Doris, set up in the outbuildings of Clarence Farm in Finchale Road, selling cigarettes to building workers, as well as sweets, tobacco, baby wool and stockings. A few days later Duncans' grocers, off right, arrived. The upstairs was used for whist drives, meetings and the amateur dramatic society (see pages 105 and 106). By 1951 there were 341 houses. Clarence Hall and Beveridge Hall community centres were built.

TEA OR COFFEE AND BUNS? Left to right: Ronnie Murray, Enid Marshall (now Mrs Hugill, see page 51), -?- and Barry Clark at Clarence Hall Community Centre, 1955.

INTERIOR, SIMPASTURE PO. Lilian Stevens is serving on the left and sister Doris busies herself below the counter. Doris married Norman Langthorn and later ran the Neville Parade shop, whilst Lilian married Ralph Holmes and had three shops. Stevens' Beveridge Way shop was to open later when the town centre was built.

STEVENS NEWSAGENTS. Ralph Holmes, Lilian's husband, created an interest in old coins. He is seen here talking to Phil Turner.

THE WHITE HOUSE. This house on the corner of Pease Way and Cumby Road was intended for Lord Beveridge. He lived from 1951, however, at 5 Bede Crescent, where he wrote much of his autobiography *Power and Influence*. He and Janet left at the end of 1952 for Edinburgh and Oxford, his chairmanship of the A.D.C. ending in 1953 after a change in government.

TREE PLANTING. A feature of the early town years was the planting of personal trees by schoolchildren. Lady Beveridge watches Michael Hiley, Mrs Pat Thompson's brother, at work. Andrew Morton, the town's horticultural officer, looks on from behind the branches.

This is to Certify
THAT
Mrs. Suddes.
Newton Aycliffe T.G
was awarded
HIGHLY COMMENDED
for Be-Ro Rice Cake
In a
BE-RO HOME BAKING
COMPETITION
held at Baths Hall, Darlington
on October 25th. 1961
Signed [illegible]
JUDGE.

Be-Ro
Self-raising FLOUR

BAKING COMPETITION, 1961. There was plenty of social activity as the New Town grew, and clubs and societies flourished. Mrs Suddes of Clarence Green and the T.W.G. was commended for her rice cake. Her husband had won a certificate of merit in 1959 in the Gardens Competition run annually by Aycliffe Development Corporation.

CHILDREN'S FILM SHOWS. Saturday film shows were also popular. This crowd outside St Clare's parish church hall is probably one such occasion. (Bill Roberts)

Above: THE FIRST BLOCK OF SHOPS, 1964. Neville Parade opened in 1952 as a neighbourhood shopping facility. Elsie Dixon remembers the early shops being Collinson, electrical goods, Newton Bakeries, Stevens PO and Duncans' groceries (both from Clarence Farm, Simpasture, see page 56), Pryce greengrocer and fruiterer, and a wet fish shop.

Left: THE POLICE SERGEANT. Jim Crawford was one of the first policemen 'on the town'. He was also one of the early management committee members of the Boys' Club. After retiring he ran a driving school in Newton Aycliffe.

THE 1,000TH HOUSE, 1953. Lord Beveridge, accompanied by Janet Lady Beveridge, unveiled a plaque at Elizabeth House, 2 Butler Road, in celebration of the coronation of Queen Elizabeth II. The young queen visited the town in 1960. (See pages 68, 69 and 90.)

THE TOWN CENTRE. The first town centre shops were opened in 1957, and Churchill House became the offices for the Development Corporation. The large roundabout had floral displays and a flagpole. Thames House and Thames Shopping Arcade were later built out over it and this view of Churchill House was thus obscured when the town centre was expanded in Phase Two. The foreground is now a car park.

AIR VIEW OF TOWN CENTRE, 1963. This A.D.C. photograph shows Central Avenue and the Avenue School with the town centre shops lined up along and across the end of Beveridge Way. Churchill House faces the large roundabout and flagpole. Beyond, there is little development as yet in the farmland around Stephenson Way. The Police Station, Magistrates Court and Greenwell Road curve are still to come, as is also the Phase Two expansion.

TOWN CENTRE SHOPPERS. Before Thames House and Arcade were built, the clock tower could be seen from Beveridge Way, which is now pedestrianized. A Tuesday open-air market was instituted here in 1979. The symbolic oak (see page 6) is on the right.

BEVERIDGE WAY. The view is south westward. Traffic had access until the town centre was extended eastwards. A plaque states that 'Town Centre Phase Two was opened by James Boyd Esq., M.P. 11th April, 1975.' A heavier style of architecture was introduced and the Way lost its sense of openness. (Bill Roberts)

SHOPS AND TRAFFIC. Well known firms on Beveridge Way include Timothy White (housewares), Carricks (confectionery), Meadow (dairy and groceries) and Dewhurst (butchers).

THE AVENUE, 1969. This snapshot shows a petrol station down the road centre before the police station was built. Gary Cook in the foreground, then aged five, is now a computer-based Information Systems Officer at Bishop Auckland Technical College. (Kenneth Cook)

BOYS' CLUB, CLINIC, LIBRARY AND OVER SIXTIES CLUB. Lord Beveridge was uneasy about the early emphasis on housing at the expense of community provision, but this did eventually come. A plaque in the library states that 'The Maternity and Child Welfare Centre and County Library building was officially opened on Wednesday, 18th September, 1963 by Alderman W. Dent, member of the Education Committee.'

Five

Events and Special Occasions

OPENING OF COUNTY POLICE HQ, 1947. Sunderland Police Band, Chief Inspector Fred Purser at the head, march past the Rt Hon. G. Chuter Ede MP at a former R.O.F. building.

OFFICIALS VISIT THE FIRST SHOP, 1951. Left to right: W.N. Davies OBE, (deputy chairman of A.D.C.), the Rt Hon. Hugh Dalton MP (Minister of Local Government and Planning), A.W. Thomas, MIMunE (general manager, A.D.C.) and Doris Stevens (now Mrs Langthorne). (See pages 56 and 57.)

LORD ROBENS VISITS U.M.M. The chairman of the National Coal Board, second left, with Heinz Asbeck, third, managing director.

NEVILLE MALE VOICE CHOIR. At an early 1950s annual dinner at The Gretna Wedding Inn, Lord Beveridge, guest of honour, is greeted by Ken Holliday, inn manager. Albert Guy, in the background with glass, has lived in the New Town from 1949, and was one of the first councillors. (The *Northern Despatch*)

GARDEN GUILD SHOW, 1958. Children surround the Revd Tom Drewette, the first vicar of St Clare's parish church. Note the first prize card held by a boy on the left. But who won it?

THE QUEEN'S VISIT, 2 MAY 1960. HM Queen Elizabeth II walks to the dais on Beveridge Way to a fanfare and guard of honour of the 6th Battalion, the Durham Light Infantry (T.A.), under Major G.W. Lear. Carolyn Corner, the first child born in the town, presented a bouquet. After signing the visitors' book, the Queen and the Duke of Edinburgh proceeded to Churchill House to an exhibition and an air view from the bell tower. (The *Northern Echo*)

A CUP OF TEA. A neighbour's snapshot captured the Queen followed by Brigadeer L.H. McRobert and, on the right, HRH Prince Philip as they walked from Simpasture Playing Field to visit Mr and Mrs William Llewellyn and their four children at 13 Barrington Road for a friendly cup of tea and fairy cakes. The royal couple explored the house and the Duke enjoyed 'Billy' Llewelyn's garden workshop with his punch and judy gear. Mr Llewelyn worked at North Road Shops and then at Shildon Wagon Works.

THE QUEEN'S VISIT. Her Majesty, in a primrose coat and matching floral dress, walks along Beveridge Way. She also visited Marlowe Hall Secondary Modern School, the RAF Association's Canopus Club, and unveiled a plaque at the new Boys' Club building. (The *Newcastle Chronicle and Journal*)

THE DUKE OF EDINBURGH'S VISIT. HRH Prince Philip visited Underground Mining Machinery Ltd. Heinz Asbeck is on the left.

A HEAT WAVE, 1959. In a very hot dry summer, Jeff and Sue Grace and cousin Derek (from left to right) enjoy a paddling pool in the garden at Lee Green. (Jim Grace)

A TOWN CENTRE FLOOD, 2 JULY 1968. At 11 a.m. the sky went dark green, and there was dreadful thunder and lightning. Harold Bell had the paint taken off the back of a brand new car in Central Avenue by lightning. (Bill Roberts)

PROLONGED SNOW, c.1976. The snapshot taken from Marley Road records six weeks of heavy snow during which time no car could be got out. Mrs Grace recalls that hedgehogs used to winter under this shed each year. (Jim Grace)

Left: SCHOOL OPEN DAY, 1968. Parents examine displays at St Mary's School Top Infants.

Below: FRANKIE VAUGHAN'S VISIT. He is at the Newton Aycliffe Boys' Club. Boys' clubs were a special interest of his.

Above: CELEBRITY CONCERT. From the left, Thomas Allen, Ann Collins and Ralph Smith were the soloists at an annual celebrity concert held by the Neville Male Voice Choir in The Avenue Comprehensive School. The choir, conductor Cyril Graham, was founded by Herbert Pryce, who opened a greengrocers shop in Neville Parade (page 60). The choir lasted for thirty years and held concerts at chapels throughout the region. Thomas Allen, trained locally, is now an internationally famous baritone.

Right: POLICEMAN'S WEDDING. PC John Gordon Bacon wed Miss Dawson.

FASHION PARADE. Ladies prepare for a fashion parade at Stevens' ladies fashions shop, showing sizes 12-24. Lilian Stevens, on the right, had the shop c.1974-81 in the town centre.

FESTIVAL, JUNE 1976. There was an exhibition in Beveridge Way, by this time pedestrianized. Note the fashionable flared trousers. (Kenneth Cook)

TOWN CARNIVAL, 1972 or 1973. The annual carnival lasted a week, a big event with a fair, an open air service, a dance to choose the Carnival Queen, open air coffee mornings in the town centre and a window-dressing competition. A procession with decorated floats by local societies and a fancy dress parade led to Simpasture Playing Field, where sports were held and judging took place. (Jim Grace)

COACH OUTING. Stevens newsagents ran an annual outing to a show in Newcastle-upon-Tyne such as *West Side Story* as a thankyou to their newspaper lads for their services. Ralph Holmes is on the coach step in Beveridge Way.

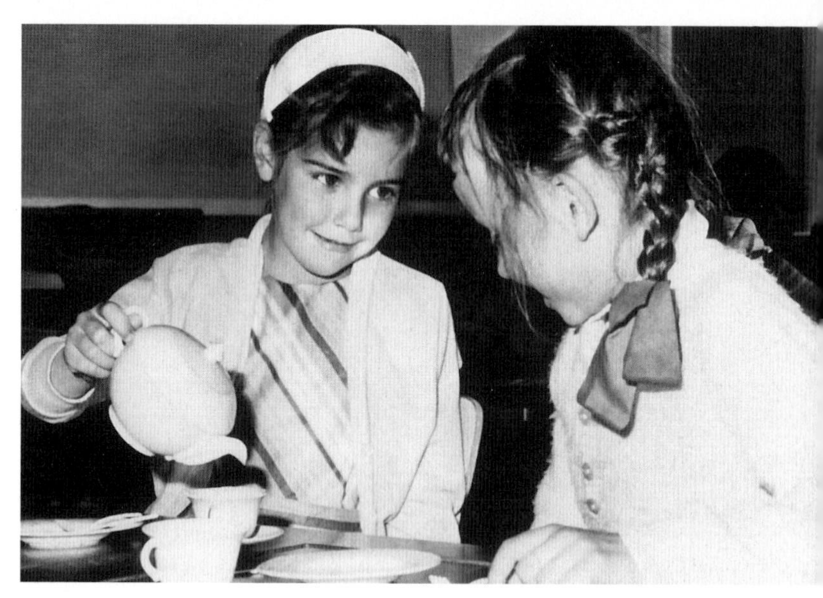

TEA FOR TWO. Play time in reception class at St Mary's RC School.

ROYAL SILVER JUBILEE, 1978. For the jubilee of Queen Elizabeth's reign a display of royal associations was put up by pupils of Vane Road County Junior School.

Above: RETIREMENT, *c*.1980. Reuben Blades, left, the first employee at Eaton Axles Ltd, retires. His wife is holding the flowers. At the centre is Ralph West (personnel manager), and on the right Madge Fitzgerald (secretary).

Right: PRIZE-GIVING. Group Captain Douglas R.S. Bader received a model Eaton Axle when he presented prizes to apprentices at Eaton's Sports and Social Club, 1980 (see page 48). He had previously opened the S.W. Durham Training Centre in 1967 (see page 41), which grew from a staff of 7 with 56 apprentices to a staff of 23 with 222 apprentices. Bader, a Second World War legend, died in 1995 whilst this book was in preparation.

Left: FREEDOM OF THE TOWN. The frigate HMS *Eskimo* was adopted by Great Aycliffe Council and the Freedom of the Town conferred on the officers and crew in 1979. The flag of the first HMS *Eskimo*, flown at the Battle of Narvick in Norway in 1940, was presented to Newton Aycliffe and is preserved in the parish church.

Below: FIRE. A part of Woodham Comprehensive School was destroyed by fire on 4 July 1990. (Bill Robson)

Six

Churches

CLARENCE FARM. This farmhouse on New Lane, Simpasture, now Finchale Road, served as the temporary church of St Clare.

Above: A SERVICE AT ST CLARE'S. The 'church' was in the bay-windowed room, where seating for forty was provided at a cost of £3 7s. 3d. by the manager of a shipyard in Hebburn. The Revd Tom Anderson Drewette, seen here, was appointed in May 1950, and the first service was held on 9 May that year. He lived at 1 Clarence Chare until a new vicarage was built.

Left: THE FIRST MARRIAGE. Thomas Punshon, 3 Anne Swift Road, and June Pearson, 5 Anne Swift Road, pose outside Clarence farmhouse church door on 16 October 1954.

Right: THE FARMHOUSE CHURCH BELL. The Revd Tom Drewette admires the Royal Navy ship's bell from HMS *Prosperine*. It cost £18 1s. 5d. and weighed two hundredweights.

Below: BAPTISM AT CLARENCE FARMHOUSE. One of the first baptisms in the parish was conducted by the Revd Tom Drewette. On the left is Joan Whitworth and her godmother and, to the right, Tony Grace with his godmother June Harker. Norman Harker is behind, the taller man is Jim Grace and Mrs Grace is on the right.

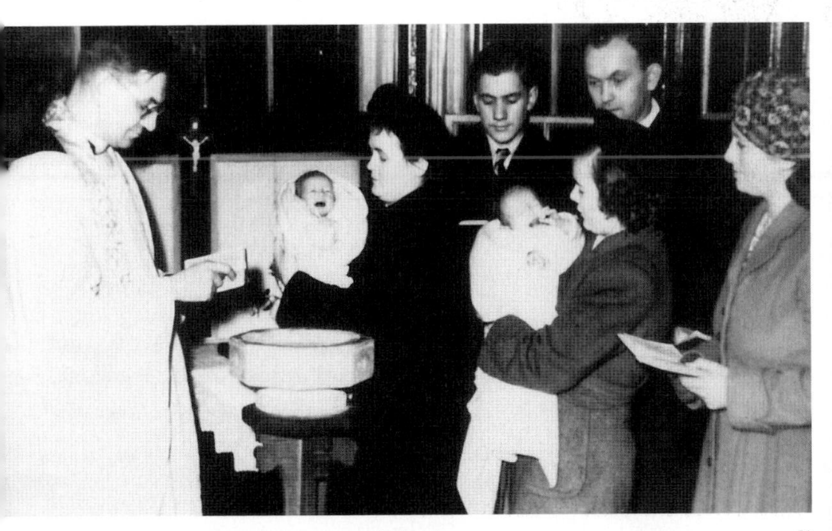

PLANNING THE NEW PARISH CHURCH. The Revd Tom Drewette and some of his congregation meet at the farmhouse to discuss a proposed new building. The BBC broadcast the discussions. The interviewer is on the left with the microphone.

THE NEW ST CLARE'S, 1955. Stanley M. Harrison remembers asking residents to sponsor bricks at 2s. 6d. per brick to raise funds. Later the church was extended forwards by two more bays (sets of windows), and a porch and verandah added to link with a parish hall and tower. In 1993 a stained glass window with a rainbow of hope and a dove of peace were inserted into the octagon window for two families who had lost young ones. More stained glass is planned for the clerestories.

DEDICATION. The new church was dedicated on 9 July 1955 by the then Bishop of Durham, the Right Reverend Michael Ramsay, who later became the Archbishop of Canterbury. The Revd Tom Drewette, on the right, died suddenly in 1961 aged 49.

FIRST WEDDING AT THE NEW CHURCH. On 16 July 1955 Eric Batchelor of 12 Greville Way married Cynthia Hugill of 7 Clarence Corner. They are photographed at Clarence farmhouse.

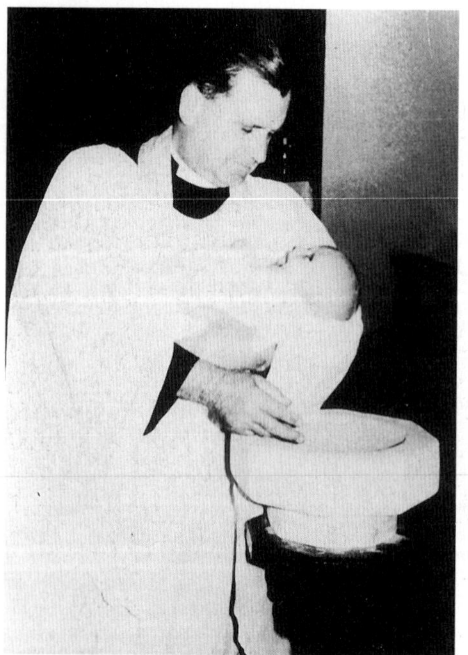

Above: A CHURCH GROUP. The Revd Tom Drewette is on the left.

Left: A CHRISTENING IN THE NEW CHURCH. The Revd John James Graham was the vicar from 1961 to 1966. During his ministry the 'mouseman' pews by Thompson of Kilburn were installed.
He died in 1979.

THE FIRST CURATE. The Revd Alan Gawith waits, right, at a wedding, with bridesmaids and choir.

'THE MAGIC VICAR.' The Revd Harold Hall, centre, vicar 1969-76, was so called for his interest in conjuring tricks and illusions. He collected antiques and ran the bric-a-brac stall at the annual sales of work. At the stall here with him are his curates Christopher Jackson and Barry Coker.

Left: THE NEXT VICAR. Granville Jackson came to Newton Aycliffe in 1977. He was a mining engineer, and had spent about four years as a team vicar at Cramlington, Northumberland. He later became Archdeacon of Durham.

Below: THE PRIMITIVE METHODIST CHURCH. A Methodist Society was founded at Simpasture in 1880. It met in railway cottages, Clarence Farm and Bluestone Cottage, until in 1919 an old railway carriage body was bought. This served until 1930 when the wooden chapel was built, seating 100 but with primitive lighting despite the electrified railway nearby. It was sited next to where the later four Simpsture shops came. The old carriage served as a vestry and tea place.

NEVILLE PARADE METHODIST CHURCH. The foundation stone for the first phase, a new large hall, was laid in 1958 by Laura Stevens (see pages 19 and 56). She is seen here with the Revd Ray Gostelon. Lady Starmer of Darlington opened it in 1959. The wooden chapel was sold and removed. The stone for the new church was laid in 1964 by Mrs W. Hydes and opened by Mrs E. Bertram, whose father had farmed this land. Clayton and Deas were the architects. (The *Northern Echo*)

BURNHILL WAY METHODIST CHURCH. Lilian Holmes (see page 57), a daughter of Laura Stevens, laid the foundation stone on 22 May 1976 at Williamfield. The Revd John Ingyon, beside her, opened the church on 11 December 1976. Lilian was christened in the old railway carriage church at Simpasture. John Wearmouth's booklet, *This from That*, details the Methodists' progress.

METHODIST HARVEST FESTIVAL CONCERT, 1953. The Neville Male Voice Choir and the Townswomen's Guild are photographed at Clarence Cottage. On the front row are Mesdames Kell, Turner and Drewette. (The *Auckland Chronicle*)

ST MARY'S RC CHURCH. At first services were held at 131 Shafto Way, a one-roomed chapel in Father O'Brian's first house. Later they were held in the Community Centre. The new church, designed by T.A. Crawford, at the corner of Central Avenue and Burn Lane, was completed in 1961, and has since been added to along the front. St Mary's Primary School was built beside it in 1963. St Joseph's RC School was built in Stephenson Way in 1970 and the church in 1984.

Seven

Schools, Teachers and Pupils

MARLOWE HALL SCHOOL, THE AVENUE. When this Secondary Modern School and the adjacent Milton Hall became comprehensive in around 1957-58 they were renamed The Avenue School. This has recently been demolished.

HEAD GIRL. Glenda Foulkes presents a bouquet to HM Queen Elizabeth II on her visit to the town's Secondary Modern School in 1960 (see pages 68, 69 and 89). By 1980 Glenda, married with two daughters and a member of St Clare's congregation, was a Girl Guides District Commissioner. (The *Northern Echo*)

THE FIRST SCHOOL IN TOWN. Sugar Hill School opened in 1953 with separate buildings and heads. Schooling had previously taken place in four converted Bede Crescent flats. These 11-plus scholarship winners of 1956 went on to the Johnson Grammar School, Durham. From the left: Ian Dobson, John Moss, -?-, Leonard Milner, Michael Brown, Alan Suddes, -?-, -?-, Eric Ainsworth and Brian Downing. The first Head was Mr Swan. Alan Suddes is the curator of Darlington Museum.

Right: A SUGAR HILL PUPIL, ATHOL HAWKES, 1953. The site, Sugar Hill Farm, had been part of the Windlestone Estate (see page 16) and was sold in 1936 to John Todd. His daughter, aged 88, attended the school's 40th Anniversary Celebrations in 1993. Fred Crusher farmed Sugar Hill before moving to Burn House.

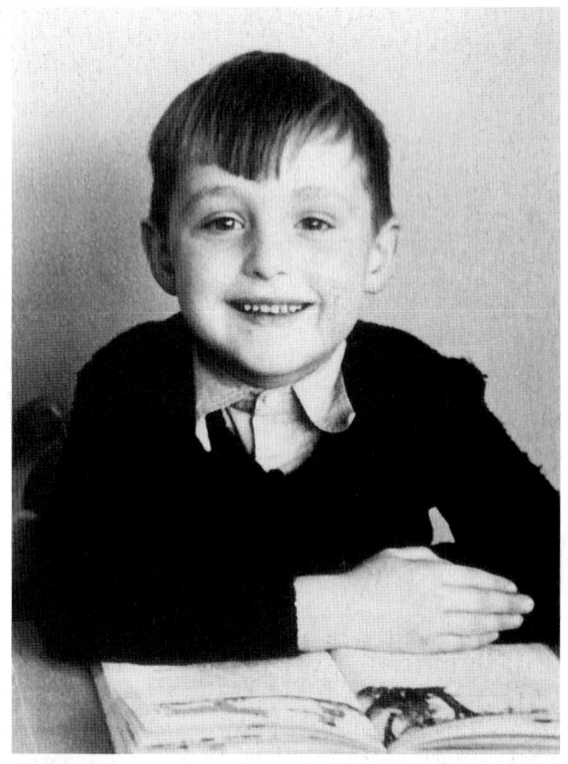

Below: CLASS 12, JUNE 1957. The teacher is Mrs Fryer. Sugar Hill Farm came to the Development Corporation in 1949 and the school to Durham County Council in 1954. The buildings were designed by G.R. Clayton, County Architect, with Grenfell Baines and Hargreaves.

SUGAR HILL'S FIRST STAFF, 1957. The Head, Ethel Milner, is centre front. Front row, second from the left is Minnie Fryer, who became the second head; fifth is Gladys Smith, the third head. The first teacher at the right end of the front row is Mary Thwaites, who came straight from college and is now Mrs Budden.

THE FIRST STUDENT TEACHERS, 1959. They came to Sugar Hill School from Darlington Training College. From the left, Anne L. Hardy, Marion Chalk, Glenda Johnston, Kathleen Callard, Pamela Banks, Una M. Archbold and Jaqueline M. Winter.

SUGAR HILL SCHOOL, 1960.

A JUNIOR GROUP, SUGAR HILL SCHOOL.

THE SAND PIT, SUGAR HILL SCHOOL.

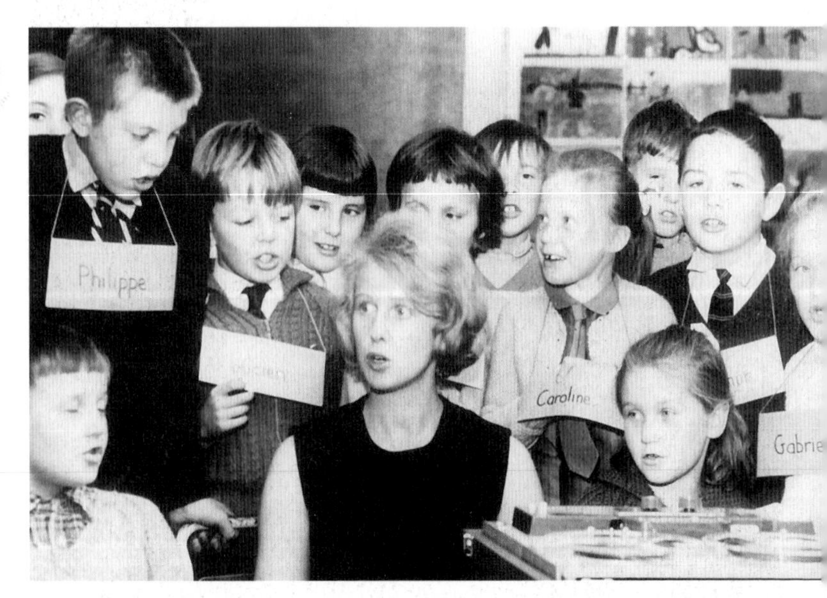

VANE ROAD SCHOOL, 1964. The school was formally opened in 1959. Barbara Cowie is seen here teaching French, a fashionable experiment in primary schools at the time. She later married Eddie Kell. (See pages 44 and 109.)

Right: ACROBATICS WINNERS, VANE ROAD SCHOOL. The Kay-Metzeler Trophy for Under-11 Girls Pairs was presented by James Lambie, managing director of Kay-Metzeler, at the English Schools Gymnastic Association's first National Sports Acrobatics Championships, sponsored by the firm.

Below: JOLLY JUNIORS, VANE ROAD SCHOOL, 1976. They had won the Tallent Engineering Ltd Road Safety Award.

VANE ROAD JUNIOR SCHOOL STAFF, EARLY 1960s. Back row, left to right: B. Stibbs, K. Gash, L. Dobson, R. Dobson and J. Thompson. Front row: A. Moore, B. Cowie, E. Hill, G. Ridley (Head), B. Blanche, -?-, ? Atkinson.

VANE ROAD JUNIOR SCHOOL STAFF, c.1981. Back row, left to right: George Courtney (international football referee), Eunice Waggett, Harry Weightman, Elizabeth Dobson, Barry Stannard, -?-, -?-. Front row, -?-, Eva Hill, Brian Stubbs (Head), -?-, Hazel Robinson.

COUNTRY DANCING, VANE ROAD JUNIOR SCHOOL, 1977. Miss Hall dances with the girls in the Queen's Silver Jubilee Year.

A SKELETON COMPETITION, VANE ROAD JUNIOR SCHOOL, 1982.

STEPHENSON WAY SCHOOL NETBALL TEAM, 1972. They won the League Championship Cup and Aycliffe Parish Shield. Back row, left to right: Linda Kelly, Carolyn Potts, Janice Strevens, Lynn Blair, Alison Cairney. Front row: W.A. Simpson (first headmaster), Avril Collings, Vicky Jones, Sally Van Linden and Miss P. Robbins.

STEPHENSON WAY SCHOOL FOOTBALL TEAM, 1967-68. They won the League Championship Shield and the Rudd Cup. Back row, left to right: A.G. Potts, C. Soulsby, L. Teder, G.J. Davison, I. Neary, M. Wilkinson, K. Turnbull. Front row: B. Wills, M.N. Young, N.D. Wilson, D.A. Simpson, K. Robinson, D. Milburn. The League and Cup were contested for in the Bishop Auckland area. The team now plays in the Newton Aycliffe League, formed as the town expanded.

ST FRANCIS C. of E. SCHOOL. (Ian Wright)

ST FRANCIS SCHOOL GOVERNORS. Back row, left to right: S.M. Harrison and F. Joyce. Front row: Deaconess Dixon, the Revd H.H. Hall (see page 85), J.C. Bainbridge, Mrs Cessford.

WOODHAM COMPREHENSIVE SCHOOL'S *CALAMITY JANE*, 1980.

WOODHAM COMPREHENSIVE SCHOOL'S *CALAMITY JANE*, 1980. The school has also performed *The Sound of Music*, *The King and I*, *Oliver*, *The Wizard of Oz* and *Oklahoma*.

WOODHAM COMPREHENSIVE SCHOOL NETBALL TEAM, 1971-72.

WHITE CUP AND DIXON SHIELD, Woodham Comprehensive School, 1976-77. Back row, left to right: Mr Golightly, Andy Morton, Mark Baxter, Tom Fisher, Wayne Shotter, Paul Kemp, Paul Mather, Stuart Howson, Peter Manson, David Curry, Lee Swainston and Mr Dunn. Front row: Lee Killip, Stephen Taylor, Kevin Cane, Paul Churchwood, Mark Howe.

ST MARY'S R.C. SCHOOL, 1962. It was opened by the Rt Revd James Cunningham, Bishop of Hexham and Newcastle, seen here on the April occasion. Sister Paul was the first Head.

THE FIRST GROUP COMMUNION, St Mary's School, 1966.

MODELS. St Mary's blue and grey school uniform is displayed for the first time.

'QUIET PLEASE.' Pupils are busy in a St Mary's School classroom.

ST MARY'S SCHOOL STAFF, 1974-75. Back row, left to right: Margaret Britten, Mary Waggott, Brian Smith, Susan Vickers and Mary Wood. Front row: Angela Eaton, Sister Joan, Sister Siobhan, John Fuller and Mary Simmons.

LEAVERS, 1970, ST MARY'S R.C. SCHOOL.

Eight

Leisure and Pleasure

THE NEWTON PLAYERS. Left to right: Ned Thompson, Amy Bell, Marjorie Spark and Derek Wood.

WHEN WE ARE MARRIED. J.B. Priestley's play was the Newton Players' fifth production. Formed in 1952 as the Newton Aycliffe Amateur Dramatic Society, they met at first in the old community hall at Clarence Farm. They presented two plays a year and a Christmas pantomime.

DANCERS' LINE-UP. Assembled at Marlowe Hall School, these are probably from Lee Green Dancing Academy.

THE RED CROSS ON THE MARCH.

RED CROSS CADETS, c.1958-59. Enid Marshall, now Mrs Hugill, was in charge of the junior contingent, but it was discontinued after she resigned. The Iron Horse was the first public house in town.

THE GARDEN SHED WHERE THE BOYS' CLUB BEGAN. Jessie Kell's four sons and their friends used to gather in her back garden shed, so she founded the Boys' Club for 11- to 21-year-olds. Premises were built in the town centre by 1960 (see page 64). The Orlitt houses in the background were of concrete slabs

JESSIE KELL WITH BOYS' CLUB MEMBERS, 1960. She was a vigorous youth leader for thirteen years, and retired in 1966. A great variety of indoor and outdoor sports, games and activities flourished, including the Duke of Edinburgh Awards. Girls were later allowed to join in.

THE KELL BROTHERS. Edward, David, Peter and Alan were the sons of Peter Kell, who came from Bishop Auckland to manage Dewhursts butchers' shop when it opened in Neville Parade. David died young. Eddie, on the right, was the enthusiastic secretary of the Boys' Club.

THE BOYS' CLUB. (See pages 122 and 123.)

FRANKIE VAUGHAN. Newton Aycliffe Boys' Club members meet with Frankie, centre back.

STARTING TO BUILD THE SCOUT HUT. This was on Finchale Road, near Clarence Farm, and is long since gone. On the left is Mr Grey, and the cub on the right is Frank Tweddle, who now teaches at Stephenson Way School. (The *Northern Echo*)

CUB AND SCOUT HUT. Complete and in use, it housed an independent pack, not attached to any church. Enid Marshall, centre, is now Mrs Hugill, Woodham Comprehensive School secretary.

WINDLESTONE CAMP SITE. Scouts line up.

CHIEF SCOUT'S PRESENTATION. Brian Winwood displays his certificate flanked by his parents, Alex and Fred Winwood, both leaders at St Clare's.

ST MARY'S R.C. SCHOOL CUB PACK.

SUE GRACE, DRUMMER, 1972-3. Sue poses in the garden of Lee Green flats in the drummer uniform of The Monarch Band. Bands took part in the annual carnival.

STEPHEN AND GILLIAN HOLMES, c.1968. They are the children of Lilian Holmes (see page 87) and grandchildren of Laura Stevens (see pages 56 and 87), and were Brigade and Brownie members at Neville Parade Methodist church. Stephen is now the sub-postmaster at Neville Parade PO.

TOWNSWOMEN'S GUILD PUBLIC SPEAKING TEAM, 1954. At the Darlington District Festival the Newton Aycliffe speakers are, from the left, Miss E.M.B. Hamilton (speaker), Mrs J.L. Kell (chairman), Mrs L. Robson (proposer of the vote of thanks), and Mrs Deane (seconder).

T.W.G. OUTING, c.1963. This is the choir section. Mrs Frank Tweddle is present.

T.W.G. DRAMA SECTION.

THE CANDLELITERS, 1967. From the left, Walter and Margaret Young, Edwina Robinson and Keith Holder in Tyne Tees TV Studio 1, 21 May 1967, in the show *Walk Right In*. They were a middle-of-the-road folk group playing English traditional and American Tom Paxton style folk songs. The Candleliters four-part harmony with acoustic guitars performed professionally from 1967 to 1979. Walter and Margaret continued for a while as a duo. Walter became a remand centre teacher, Edwina is in Hong Kong, and Keith is a fireman in Middlesbrough. (Photograph Tyne Tees TV)

THE OPERATIC SOCIETY'S *THE MERRY WIDOW*, 1968. The principals are Janice Towns (Anna), Robert Sowerby (Danilo), Gerhard Pretzel (Baron Zeta), Rita Bamford (Valencienne), Ron Wells (Camille) and David Thompson (Njegus). The Society began in 1963 and ended in 1994. Their first show was *The Mikado*.

THE OPERATIC SOCIETY'S *THE PALACE OF VARIETIES*, 1972. The soloists are, from the left, Janice Towns, Vera Davison, Joy Raisbeck and Nancy Jude. (Galdon, Tow Law)

Right: THE OPERATIC SOCIETY'S *THE VAGABOND KING*, 1976. The Principals are Vince Vickers, Janice Towns, Vera Davison and Cec. Jones. Other productions included *The Gondoliers* and *Ruddigore*. (Galdon, Tow Law)

Below: THE OPERATIC SOCIETY'S *THE VAGABOND KING*, 1976. The chorus poses. There was also a Newton Aycliffe Music Society which arranged professional concerts for many years in co-operation with Darlington Music Society.

GARDEN GUILD ANNUAL SHOW, 1960s. Heinz Asbeck, U.M.M. Ltd, presents the U.M.M.-Greenside Company Trophy.

OUTING TO REDCAR, c.1960. The ladies were a part of U.M.M.'s whole firm outing. Back row, on the left, Lisel Asbeck.

A QUIET DRINK? Members of Aycliffe Development Corporation have a chat. Left to right: Andrew Morton (chief horticultural officer), -?-, Frank Hiley (chief finance officer) and Bill Thomas (general manager).

CANOES ON WEST PARK LAKE, SIMPASTURE. The lake was created c.1971, and the banks grassed and planted with trees. (David Angles)

LABOUR PARTY, WOMEN'S SECTION. Behind the banner, centre, is Jessie Kell. (The *Auckland Chronicle*)

BUS PRESERVATION SOCIETY. The society was formed in 1980 to restore vintage buses. This bus, GHN 189, was new in 1942. The original body was replaced in 1949 with an Eastern coachworks body. It was sold in 1959 to Silcox of Pembroke Dock, withdrawn from service in 1969, sold in 1970 for scrap and restored by the Society. (Information courtesy of John Gibson, Gordon Hollis, the PVS Circle and the Omnibus Society)

Nine

Sport

THE FIRST CRICKET TEAM, 1954. Back row, left to right: Enid Marshall (scorer), Arthur Rowell, ? Hood, -?-, -?-, ? Scarlett, ? Bedward. Front row: ? Mulholland,-?-, ? Burton, -?-, -?-, -?-.

U.M.M. TEAM.

NEWTON AYCLIFFE UNDER-18s FOOTBALL TEAM, 1967. Durham County Council Association of Boys' Clubs final at Murton Welfare Ground between Newton Aycliffe and Cleveland Hall, Gateshead. Back row, left to right: J. Vickers, S. Langley, W. Robson, G. Reed, J. Coates and A. Kell. Front row: D. Lovelass, K. Bibby, J. Graham, K. Summers, I. Melvin.

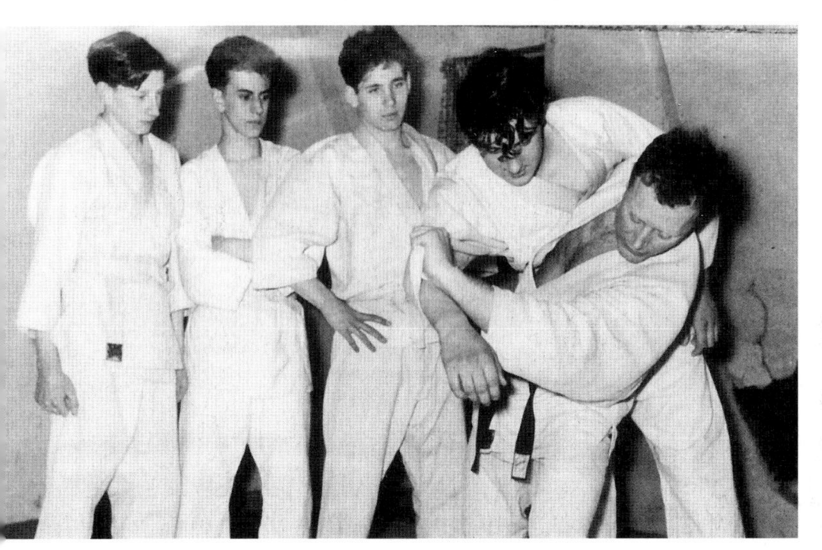

JUDO. Newton Aycliffe Boys' Club practise, probably before 1966, the year when the Youth Leader Mrs Kell retired.

ATHLETICS. The team at Newton Aycliffe Boys' Club.

THE PARISH SHIELD, 1969. The first winners of the shield presented by the parish council at an inter-schools tournament were a team from St Mary's. Those shown are M. Harty, L. Harrington, M. Taylor, C. Brown, E. Walker (reserve), J. Lee, S. Edwards, C. Dillon.

THE FIRST TEAM, ST MARY'S SCHOOL, 1966.

HOCKEY TEAM, WOODHAM COMPREHENSIVE SCHOOL, 1972

ATHLETICS TEAM, VANE ROAD JUNIOR SCHOOL, 1976.

FOOTBALL CAPTAINS. The head at Woodham Burn School looks on as the captains of Woodham Close and Sugar Hill Schools teams shake hands before the game. (Sonny Steele)

GYMNASTICS TEAM, 1975-76. Vane Road Junior School Team pose with their cups.

SPORTS COMPETITORS, ST MARY'S SCHOOL, 1973.

OAK LEAF SPORTS COMPLEX. Members of a coaching course for youngsters pause in the Indoor Sports Complex. Set in 109 acres of playing fields and a golf course, the complex was opened in 1978 by HRH The Prince of Wales.

Acknowledgements

My grateful thanks go to those who have allowed me to copy and discuss their photographs, and helped me in my search. I have been careful to establish ownership and ensure permission to reproduce. If there are any errors or omissions, I do apologise. Photographers, where known, are named beside their photographs.

Substantial contributions have been made by Great Aycliffe Town Council, St. Clare's Parish Church, Sugar Hill, Vane Road, St. Mary's, and Stephenson Way Primary Schools, Woodham Comprehensive, Eaton Ltd., Lilian Holmes, Eddie Kell, Athol Hawkes, Rene Grace, Lisel Asbeck and Eric Lodge.

Other contributors and helpers are
Mollie and David Angles, the Revd Peter A. Baldwin, Alex Bell, Nora Brewster, Kath Briggs, Walter Cadd, Mrs Callaby, Stan Cavell, Loreen Chadwick, Edna Chippendale,
Judith Collinson, John Cook, Kenneth Cook, Ella Crabtree, Mr Crowther, Fred Crusher,
Mr E.S. Dixon, Elsie Dixon, Harold Doran, Janet English, Johnathan Evans, John D. Fisher, Chris Forster, Stella Fowler, John F. Gibson, Betty Gunter, Albert Guy, Ben Hardaker,
Mr Hardy, Alf Hart, Jennie Harrison, Doreen Head, Gordon L. Hollis, Stephen Holmes,
Syd Howarth (Newton Press), Enid Hugill, Ann Hutchinson, Ralph Hymer, Edith Johnson, Doris Langthorne, Mrs B. Little, Billy Llewelyn, Bernadette McCormick, Mary Murphy,
Joe and Laura Nattrass, Gladys O'Connor, Mrs E. Proud, Elaine Questa, Linda Ramsay,
Roma Reed, Susan Reed, Dorothy Richardson, Sylvia Rowland, David Royle, George Scott, Fred H. Smith, PC Bill Smith, Marjorie Spark, Tom Spowart, Alan Suddes, John Temple,
Pat Thompson, Laura Thornton, Kenneth W. Tinkler, Ruth Toothill, Janice Towns,
Frank Tweddle, Edna Vickers, John Wearmouth, W. H. Williams, Alex and Fred Winwood and Walter and Margaret Young.

Beamish The North of England Open Air Museum, Darlington Museum, The Chief Constable of Durham, Durham County Council Arts, Libraries and Museums Service, *Newcastle Chronicle and Journal Ltd*, and North of England Newspapers have also allowed their photographs to be included.